NEW HAMPSHIRE

Megan Kopp

LET'S READ

AV²
BY WEIGL™

ADDED VALUE · AUDIO VISUAL

Go to **www.av2books.com**, and enter this book's unique code.

BOOK CODE

N634560

AV² by Weigl brings you media enhanced books that support active learning.

AV² provides enriched content that supplements and complements this book. Weigl's AV² books strive to create inspired learning and engage young minds in a total learning experience.

Your AV² Media Enhanced books come alive with...

Audio
Listen to sections of the book read aloud.

Video
Watch informative video clips.

Embedded Weblinks
Gain additional information for research.

Try This!
Complete activities and hands-on experiments.

Key Words
Study vocabulary, and complete a matching word activity.

Quizzes
Test your knowledge.

Slide Show
View images and captions, and prepare a presentation.

... and much, much more!

Published by AV² by Weigl
350 5th Avenue, 59th Floor
New York, NY 10118
Website: www.av2books.com   www.weigl.com

Library of Congress Cataloging-in-Publication Data
Kopp, Megan.
 New Hampshire/ Megan Kopp.
   p. cm. -- (Explore the U.S.A.)
 Includes bibliographical references and index.
 ISBN 978-1-61913-377-8 (hard cover : alk. paper)
 1. New Hampshire--Juvenile literature. I. Title.
 F34.3.K67 2012
 974.2--dc23
                          2012015606

Printed in the United States of America in North Mankato, Minnesota
1 2 3 4 5 6 7 8 9 16 15 14 13 12

052012
WEP040512

Project Coordinator: Karen Durrie
Art Director: Terry Paulhus

Weigl acknowledges Getty Images as the primary image supplier for this title.

NEW HAMPSHIRE

Contents

3

This is New Hampshire.
It is called the Granite State.
Granite is a rock found in New Hampshire.

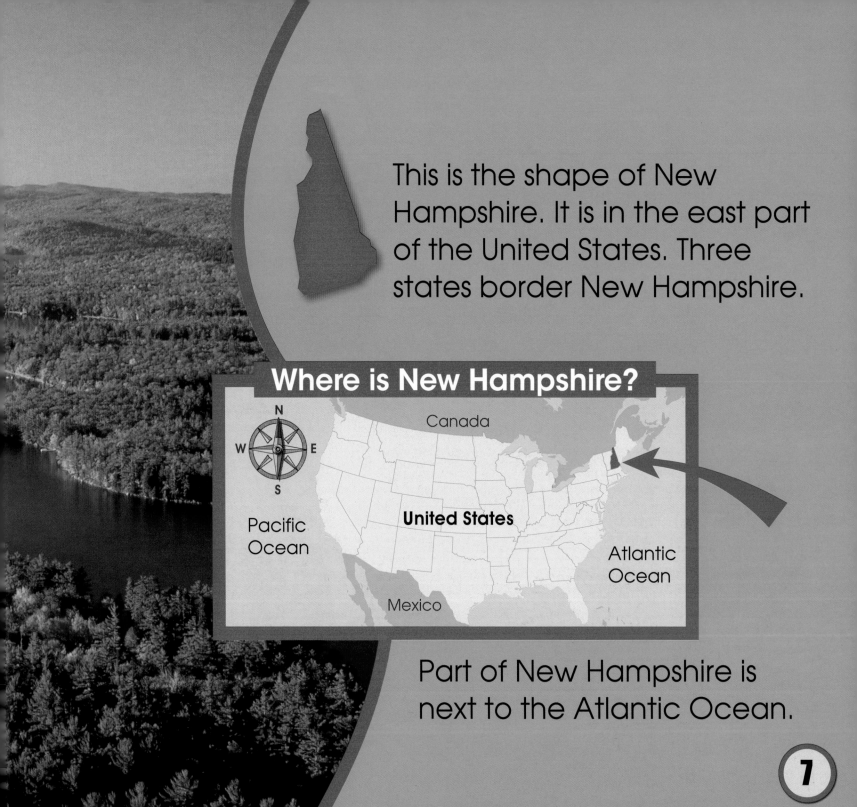

This is the shape of New Hampshire. It is in the east part of the United States. Three states border New Hampshire.

Where is New Hampshire?

Canada

N
W E
S

Pacific Ocean

United States

Atlantic Ocean

Mexico

Part of New Hampshire is next to the Atlantic Ocean.

England once owned New Hampshire. English settlers cleared land and built houses to make towns. Portsmouth, Dover, and Exeter were the first big towns.

Many people came from England to settle in New Hampshire.

The purple lilac is the New Hampshire state flower. A lilac cluster has many tiny flowers.

The New Hampshire state seal has a ship and a rising Sun.

The ship was one of the first warships in the United States Navy.

This is the state flag of New Hampshire. It is blue and has the state seal.

The seal has leaves and stars around it.

The state animal of New Hampshire is the white-tailed deer. These deer can jump up to 9 feet in the air.

White-tailed deer can swim 13 miles an hour.

This is the capital city of New Hampshire. It is named Concord. More than 42,000 people live in Concord.

The Library of Congress in Washington, D.C. was made from Concord granite.

New Hampshire has many apple trees. More than 42 kinds of apples grow in New Hampshire.

Bees help apple blossoms turn into apples.

New Hampshire has woodlands, waterfalls, and many covered bridges.

People visit New Hampshire to enjoy nature and learn about history.

NEW HAMPSHIRE FACTS

These pages provide detailed information that expands on the interesting facts found in the book. These pages are intended to be used by adults as a learning support to help young readers round out their knowledge of each state in the *Explore the U.S.A.* series.

Pages 4–5

Granite is a hard, gray stone found throughout New Hampshire. New Hampshire once had a large granite quarrying industry. The state is also called the "Mother of Rivers" because the rivers in the region start in New Hampshire's mountains. Captain John Mason named the state after Hampshire, England.

Pages 6–7

On June 21, 1788, New Hampshire became the ninth state to join the United States. It is one of six New England states . New Hampshire borders Vermont, Maine, and Massachusetts. The state shares its northern border with Canada. New Hampshire's 13-mile (21-kilometer) southeast coastline on the Atlantic Ocean is the shortest of any state that borders an ocean.

Pages 8–9

The first recorded exploration of New Hampshire was in 1603. Eleven years later, Captain John Smith mapped the area for England. Small groups of European settlers soon sailed across the ocean to make a new life in the colony. When the American Revolution began in 1775, soldiers from New Hampshire took up arms against Great Britain and battled for independence. In 1776, New Hampshire was the first colony to adopt its own constitution.

Pages 10–11

The purple lilac was made the state flower in 1919. It won a vote over several other flowers because its hardy nature was believed to symbolize the character of the citizens of New Hampshire. The ship on the seal is the frigate *Raleigh*. The boat was built in New Hampshire in 1776, the year the state gained independence.

New Hampshire's state flag shows the state seal surrounded by laurel leaves and nine stars on a field of blue. Laurel leaves symbolize victory and peace. The nine gold stars represent New Hampshire as the ninth state to join the Union.

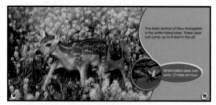

The white-tailed deer weighs between 100 and 300 pounds (45 and 136 kilograms). White-tailed deer are fast runners, capable of traveling up to 30 miles (48 kilometers) per hour. More than 85,000 white-tailed deer live in New Hampshire. Other animals found in the state include snowshoe hares, beavers, black bears, moose, porcupines, and bobcats.

Concord was first settled in 1727 along the banks of the Merrimack River. The village was incorporated into Massachusetts in 1773 and was called Rumford. It was renamed Concord when it became part of New Hampshire in 1765. Concord became the New Hampshire capital city in 1808.

Apples are an important crop in New Hampshire. McIntosh, Cortland, and Baldwin apples are grown in the state. There are about 50 apple orchards in New Hampshire. For an apple blossom to become an apple, it must be cross-pollinated. This means the pollen from one flower must land on another. Bees take pollen from flower to flower.

The White Mountain National Forest has more visitors each year than Yellowstone and Yosemite National Parks combined. People camp, bike, and climb in the forest. New Hampshire has 54 covered bridges. The oldest covered bridge in the state is more than 180 years old. The covered bridges are protected by state law.

KEY WORDS

Research has shown that as much as 65 percent of all written material published in English is made up of 300 words. These 300 words cannot be taught using pictures or learned by sounding them out. They must be recognized by sight. This book contains 52 common sight words to help young readers improve their reading fluency and comprehension. This book also teaches young readers several important content words, such as proper nouns. These words are paired with pictures to aid in learning and improve understanding.

Page	Sight Words First Appearance
4	a, found, in, is, it, state, the, this
7	of, part, three, to, where
8	and, big, came, first, from, houses, land, make, many, once, people, were
11	has, one, was
12	around, leaves
15	air, an, animal, can, feet, miles, these, up
16	city, live, made, more, named, than
19	grow, help, into, kinds, trees, turn
20	about, learn

Page	Content Words First Appearance
4	granite, New Hampshire, rock
7	Atlantic Ocean, shape, United States
8	Dover, England, Exeter, Portsmouth, settlers, towns
11	cluster, flower, lilac, navy, seal, ship, Sun
12	flag, stars
15	hour, white-tailed deer
16	Concord, Library of Congress, Washington, D.C.
19	apples, bees, blossoms
20	bridges, history, nature, waterfalls, woodlands

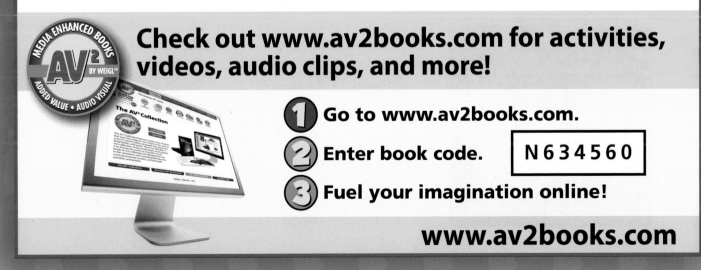